MW01504151

Commentary On Genesis

Volume 3

Discussions In Scripture Series

A Creationist Commentary

By Pastor Steven Waldron

Publishing assistance by BookCrafters, Parker, Colorado.
www.bookcrafters.net

An Introduction

THIS IS NOT A MODERN TYPE of Biblical Commentary. Rather, it hearkens back to a time of Scriptural discussions on a popular level from a bygone era. It is an attempt to lift out of Scripture the truths God intended, both in the immediate context and in an applicatory sense. It also does not attempt to answer every question and nuance that Scripture presents. On the essentials it is absolute, such as the Deity of Jesus, monotheism, salvation, holiness, and the character of God. But there are certain ancillary things that very good men disagree on. Paul spoke of days and meats as being some of those issues in Romans 14. According to John 21, the early Church had a rumor that John would not die until Jesus would come back. So, there was latitude on certain things in the early Church. And such there should be today. There is an old saying, "In the essentials unity, in the non-essentials liberty, in all things charity." Now determining what is essential is paramount. God put it like this in Deuteronomy 29:29, "The secret things belong unto the LORD our God: but those things which are revealed belong unto us and to our children for ever, that we may do all the words of this law." Major, essential doctrines will be presented, with other views sometimes offered, and occasionally refuted. Certain issues, such as the identity of the sons of God in Genesis, will be looked at from various viewpoints, but a definitive conclusion may not be proffered. So, we will be discussing Holy Scripture. There is no higher or more important level of discussion that we can have. Oh, that Scripture was on every lip and tongue throughout the world!

Matthew Henry, Thomas Scott, Matthew Poole, Charles Spurgeon, Charles Wesley, and D.L. Moody are among Biblical expositors in times past that would have used a similar style of engagement with Holy Writ. Truth will be presented. However, it may not always be buttressed with the full weight of apologetic argumentation. This present series seeks to be a truthful, honest handling of God's Holy Word in reverence and great care. But it intends on being eminently readable as well. Something to be read enjoyably, as well as a reference work. All evidence for every viewpoint by necessity will not be given. Breadcrumbs may be dropped, handfuls on purpose, to lead to a deeper discovery of truth.

I would be remiss if I did not mention the great mentors and teachers God has so graciously imparted into my life. Dr. Samuel Latta, the great Missionary Evangelist was my Pastor. He died when I was writing this, in the summer of 2019. He will be sorely missed, not just by me, but by the world at large. His passion for Divine Truth is exhilarating. His father, Thomas Latta - Church Planter and Bible expositor nonpareil, had a deep and lasting impact on my life. Sister Ruby Martin of Jackson College of Ministries, and her love of Scripture, was infectious. Pastor Thomas Craft, Dr. David Bernard, Pastor Darrell Johns, Pastor David Reever, Rev. Alan Oggs, Pastor Jonathan Urshan, Pastor Paul Mooney, Pastor Nathaniel Wilson, Pastor Johnny Godair, Pastor Larry Booker, and Rev. O.C. Marler have all sharpened the sword of Scripture in my life in various ways, and for that I am forever grateful. Other ministries and books too countless and laborious to name form a tapestry in my life. The veil of blue, purple, scarlet, cherubim's, and fine twined linen has been sewn warp and woof into my life through them. Without them, and how God used them, my life would in some sense be incomplete. Complete in Jesus yes, but God used them as well. Helpful resources will be mentioned as are deemed appropriate.

The goal is to have a truthful look at each passage of Scripture. Of the making of books there is no end according to Solomon. The world itself could not contain the books that should be written about Jesus. So, it is impossible to flesh each nugget from every jot and tittle of Scripture. Truth, and God's essential revelation is the desired goal. "How can I understand except some man teach me" was a paraphrased cry of the Ethiopian Eunuch. We should study to show ourselves approved unto God, rightly dividing the word of truth.

The Scripture is the mind of God. It has been with God throughout all eternity. He has graciously revealed and preserved it to mankind. Within its pages are life. They testify of Jesus. What greater thing is there to discuss? So, pull up a chair, and with prayerful, reverent, holy awe, let us see how we can apply God's revealed will to our lives, shall we?

I will not follow current grammatical guidelines concerning capitalization of certain sacred subjects. I will capitalize what I feel is sacred, regardless of current conventions of English. That is my prerogative.

Discussions in Scripture 3
Chapters 12b and 13

IN CASE YOU HAVE NOT READ the previous two volumes, that is quite alright. This is a stand alone Commentary, which may on occasion refer back to previous volumes, but will be readily understandable without access to the other books. I do need to mention a couple of things, however.

First, rules of grammar in regards to Deity, Scripture and such like, will not necessarily follow accepted norms. Capitalizations will be used out of respect and honor in many cases where it may not necessarily be generally accepted. The same can go for lower case usage as well. The differences will be easy to see, and will not interrupt reading and study.

Secondly, I will be giving recommendations on resources, and if I am directly quoting a source, I will, of course acknowledge that. I will not be using footnotes, however. Any acknowledgements of sources will be found in the text itself. I have found that is the most beneficial to me personally in books I have read, and is also the most time efficient way to write.

So much of the Chronology used will be from Ussher, with occasional nods to Reese or Jones. I will try to continually remind the reader of that.

Let's begin. We here find Abram, as he and his entourage are in dire straits in Egypt. They have gone to Egypt because of famine. Sarai is in the midst of being taken captive by Pharaoh, but Pharaoh is giving to Abram due to Abram's duplicity, rather than killing him to obtain Sarai. We pick up the Scripture in Genesis 12:16, and the year is around 1921 BC. Reese, in the Reese Chronological Study Bible, informs us that the 430 year sojourn in Egypt began in 1921 BC, and ended in 1491 BC, after 215 years in Canaan and 215 years in Egypt. Canaan was controlled by Egypt during this time. He gives the distance from Bethel to Memphis at 303 miles, which was Abram's journey. He also says the Pharaoh during this time was Senusret/ Sesostris 1 who ruled from 1950-1878 BC. With that as a backdrop, **Genesis 12:16** reads:

"And he entreated Abram well for her sake: and he had sheep, and oxen, and he asses, and menservants, and maidservants, and she asses, and camels."

We notice in 12:15 that Sarai was taken to Pharaoh's house, not palace. Being so soon after the dispersion at Babel, quite possibly Egypt was still developing as a dynastic, monarchial power.

Pharaoh begins to dole quite a bit of wealth to Abram. Abram already had a seemingly substantial amount of wealth already. This, of course is in God's plan for him. This would probably be where Abram would obtain Hagar.

Genesis 12:17 "And the LORD plagued Pharaoh and his house with great plagues because of Sarai Abram's wife."

430 years later, God would once again plague Pharaoh's land. Since from Sarai would come the future Messiah, it was of utmost importance in God's economy to rescue Sarai. We don't know what these great plagues were. It is somewhat of a theme in this mid-part of Genesis that God was actively involved in protecting Abram and his chosen seed's brides.

Getting back to plagues, of course the 10 plagues in Exodus are quite famous, as are the plagues on the Philistines concerning the Ark of the Covenant in 1 Samuel. Plagues are rather ubiquitous in Revelation. Various plagues would strike throughout Israel's history.

Concerning the plagues here mentioned, the identity of them must not be that important to us, since God chose not to include them in Holy Writ. But the fact that He did plague Pharaoh and his house because of Sarai is important.

Genesis 12:18 And Pharaoh called Abram, and said, What is this that thou hast done unto me? why didst thou not tell me that she was thy wife?

We're not sure how Pharaoh and his household correlated the plagues with the fact of Sarai being married. We are also not told if there was any indiscretions involved between Sarai and Pharaoh. But it was found out that the reason for the plagues was the fact that Sarai was married. Throughout Genesis and Job, the two earliest Books of the Bible, we see how adultery and sex outside of marriage was frowned upon strongly during this time period. Even among people who were not Hebrews. It is recorded in Job that it was actually a civil crime, "For this is an heinous crime; yea, it is an iniquity to be punished by the judges." Job 31:11. Reading the Constitutions of the American Colonies, many of them would certainly concur.

Genesis 12:19 "Why saidst thou, She is my sister? so I might have taken her to me to wife: now therefore behold thy wife, take her, and go thy way."

Whether there is a semblance of moral righteousness in Pharaoh, or the plagues had been so severe it convinced him to return Sarai, it is difficult to fully ascertain. The significance of this action concerning the Promises of God, and the future salvation of the human race cannot be overlooked.

Genesis 12:20 "And Pharaoh commanded his men concerning him: and they sent him away, and his wife, and all that he had."

Again, the severity of the plagues must have been such that Pharaoh did not ask for his goods back that he had given to Abram.

Genesis 13:1 "And Abram went up out of Egypt, he, and his wife, and all that he had, and Lot with him, into the south.

Egypt being southwest of Canaan, Abram's entourage migrates up, or back north. The previous few years of Abram and his group had been one of much travelling. Archaeology is still discovering the vast trade routes that existed by land and sea around this area at this time. It is quite a bit more expansive than previously thought, so Abram's journeys would not seem too out of the ordinary. The normal concerns of thieves, provision, and predators would have been a concern. And in this case, they were going back were they had just left because of famine. Faith in God's Word was all Abram had. His faith had action. He obeyed the voice of God, and it was accounted as faith to him. We are not certain the time of year these journeys of Abram would have taken place.

Genesis 13:2 "And Abram was very rich in cattle, in silver, and in gold"

Gold was considered precious as far back as the Garden of Eden. It is fascinating how silver and gold became a medium of exchange, and was recognized as having worth and value. I would say it must have been something communicated to Adam by God, or Adam just knew it being in God's image. The New Jerusalem is made out of gold, so God put gold here on earth, and it has intrinsic value. Silver less so. Silver traditionally has had about 1/15th the value of gold.

Abram is described as very rich. He would live close to another century from this point. Cattle, or domesticated farm animals, were recognized as part of his wealth. It was something God could bless with multiplication and health.

Since we now have a better covenant, based upon better promises (though Hebrews is contrasting the Old Covenant with the New Covenant in Hebrews in the aforementioned point) many feel we should be rich like Abram. Some NT Scriptures used to buttress this thinking are:

"For ye know the grace of our Lord Jesus Christ, that, though he was rich, yet for your sakes he became poor, that ye through his poverty might be rich." 2 Corinthians 8:9

"Beloved, I wish above all things that thou mayest prosper and be in health, even as thy soul prospereth." 3 John 2.

Some obvious issues with this position is the fact that the Apostles and the early Church never experienced this as recorded in the NT. And they are the arbiters of Truth and what we should ascribe to attain to as our pattern. It is not to say riches are wrong. But we should seek Jesus, not riches. Seek ye first is the admonition of Jesus. God can and does prosper His people. Paul appeals to this multiple times in encouraging giving in the NT. But not everyone will be unimaginably rich in material things in this life. Spiritually we can be however, through the Baptism of the Holy Ghost and the New Birth experience.

As the narrative progresses, we will see how Abram's wealth will play a role in several episodes in his life.

Genesis 13:3 "And he went on his journeys from the south even to Bethel, unto the place where his tent had been at the beginning, between Bethel and Hai;"

Abram goes back to his altar and where it is last recorded he called on God (12:8). This, of course, seems to have obvious significance, but really, we could only speculate on the exact nature or natures of that signification. Camping between the house of God (Bethel) and ruin (Ai) of course could be instructive as well.

Romans 8:28 certainly seemed to be working in Abram's life. Even when he makes unwarranted decisions, it seems he still comes out blessed. However, if Egypt is where he acquired Hagar, there would be future tension predicated on his decisions. We make our decisions, and our decisions make us. We have freedom, but we are not free from consequences.

Genesis 13:4 "Unto the place of the altar, which he had made there at the first: and there Abram called on the name of the LORD."

Sometimes we need to go back to the place we last called on God. Now Abram may have built several altars after his first excursion from Bethel, but it is not recorded. If he did not, but the argument from silence, of course, is not conclusive, he was coming back for a right relationship with God possibly. He had lied. He did not have the New Birth as we do now. He went back to the altar and called on God. Maybe the false gods of Egypt grieved him. Or maybe he was just familiar with the area, or possibly a confluence of factors caused him to go back there. But he went. We would be wise to do the same, Bethel, the House of God.

With the added wealth of Egypt, Abram's blessing would quite probably begin to be unwieldy. Provision and protection for such an entourage would be increasingly burdensome.

Calling on the name of the One who had called him. Abram vocalized the Name of Jehovah, the Hashem (Name). Calling on God's Name will play a major role throughout Scripture. You cannot be saved without doing so (Acts 2:21; Romans 10:9; 1 Corinthians 12:3 among others).

Fascinatingly the altar evidently had not been torn down. It does say the place of the altar, and not the altar itself, so I guess the possibility exists that the altar was gone, but it could just be a turn of phrase.

When one has been a sojourner like Abram, an altar is a wellspring of stability.

Genesis 13:5 "And Lot also, which went with Abram, had flocks, and herds, and tents."

Lot, Abram's nephew, had accumulated various forms of wealth also. The mention that he had tents indicates that he had family, workers, or both, or he had tents to carry supplies in. Whatever the case or combination thereof, a seminal moment is coming in the biography of Abram here in Genesis.

Genesis 13:6 "And the land was not able to bear them, that they might dwell together: for their substance was great, so that they could not dwell together."

The portion of Canaan they were in was not large enough to hold the combined family wealth of Abram and Lot. We must remember that there were other people groups in the land as well, far more established than these two Mesopotamian nomads. Water, pasture, and size constraints made a dwelling together of the two families untenable.

Genesis 13:7 "And there was a strife between the herdmen of Abram's cattle and the herdmen of Lot's cattle: and the Canaanite and the Perizzite dwelled then in the land."

Both Lot and Abram had hired servants. There were various classifications of servants throughout the ANE (Ancient Near East), from what we would consider employees, to near family members with certain family rights, to the horrific trauma of slavery, and other designations between. Abram and Lot's herdmen would be arguing over grazing rights, water, and possibly the mixture of their herds.

There is much speculation on the mention of the Canaanite and the Perizzite being in the land. The most natural interpretation seems to me to be that these groups, probably being larger and more established in the land, would seize on any disunity between Abram and Lot to divide and conquer. Possibly the unified force of Lot and Abram with their entourage would be large enough to discourage encroachment. Tension between Abram and Lot's servants would be a dangerous precursor to possible attack.

Others feel that Abram and Lot's God-fearing witness would be hindered by the disagreement. There is quite possibly an element of that, especially with Abram being at the altar by Bethel, the house of God.

This is the first of 23 mentions of Perizzites in Scripture. They extend chronologically from this time to the timeframe of Ezra and Nehemiah. Their name means dweller in villages.

Genesis 13:8 "And Abram said unto Lot, Let there be no strife, I pray thee, between me and thee, and between my herdmen and thy herdmen; for we be brethren."

Abram being the uncle takes the lead to diffuse the situation. He is about to offer the low road in humility, letting Lot choose the place of dwelling even though it was he that had the promise of God.

Following peace with all men is Biblical. Blessed are the peacemakers for they shall be called the children of God. Abram recognized the importance of maintaining peace in a family environment. The term brethren in this Verse refers to close male family members.

Genesis 13:9 "Is not the whole land before thee? separate thyself, I pray thee, from me: if thou wilt take the left hand, then I will go to the right; or if thou depart to the right hand, then I will go to the left."

Abram probably had the legal rights in the filial traditions of the day to be able to dictate the terms. Again, he shows his humility by allowing his nephew to choose the land he would dwell in. It would be a faithful choice indeed.

Genesis 13:10 "And Lot lifted up his eyes, and beheld all the plain of Jordan, that it was well watered every where, before the LORD destroyed Sodom and Gomorrah, even as the garden of the LORD, like the land of Egypt, as thou comest unto Zoar."

This was obviously Moses adding the commentary through inspiration that Jehovah would destroy Sodom and Gomorrah. Moses was looking back upon the event, but also knew what it was like before the destruction through Divine Inspiration. Moses also wandered for 40 years somewhat close to where Sodom and Gomorrah would have once been. Possibly nomadic tales had been told him of the situation both before and after. And being learned of all the learning in Egypt, Sodom and Gomorrah may have been part of the curriculum being located so close by.

Lot saw that the plain of the Jordan River was well watered everywhere. They had recently experienced famine and water shortage, possibly still occurring. Lot was making a shrewd business decision. Egypt's climate during this period, with the receding ice age from the Flood, was much more conducive to vegetation growth. It would have been cooler and less arid. Notice reference is made back to the Garden of Eden as a historical place, and not symbolic.

Genesis 13:11 "Then Lot chose him all the plain of Jordan; and Lot journeyed east: and they separated themselves the one from the other."

This part of Canaan must have been fairly sparse in population, at least for nomadic pursuits. Most of the population must have lived in the five cities of the plain. This also lets us see that Canaan in general was not densely populated. The population was still expanding after the dispersal from Babel some 300+ years before.

So Lot chose all the plain of Jordan. This statement once again reveals the lack of population in the area. Seeing these two family members and their households separate from one another, after hundreds of miles of travel and years together, is really quite staggering. Will Lot be able to lead his household properly without the prayerful hand of Abram? That is a question that we will see the answer unfold in the next few chapters. It was Abram who built the altars and called on the Name of the LORD, not Lot, or at least not that is recorded in Scripture.

Genesis 13:12 "Abram dwelled in the land of Canaan, and Lot dwelled in the cities of the plain, and pitched his tent toward Sodom."

Though Lot had much goods leading to his severance with Abram, he chose to dwell in cities. Sodom was well known for its immorality even at this date (Verse 13). We could only speculate for Lot's possible desire to dwell in cities rather than continue the Bedouin lifestyle he had been in. Possibly the famine led to his desire to be in a more fruitful, stable place. The phrase, "pitched his tent toward Sodom" has entered the lexicon of Christianity as going toward immorality. His direction determined his destination. He eventually ended up in the city gate of Sodom.

The Ebla Tablets mention Sodom, Gomorrah, and the Cities of the Plain. Sodom is currently thought to be Tel-el-Hammam, or possibly buried underneath the Dead Sea. A pillar is still in the area commonly referred to as Lot's wife.

Genesis 13:13 "But the men of Sodom were wicked and sinners before the LORD exceedingly."

Genesis 19 and Ezekiel 16:49 describe the sins of Sodom. A particular sin still bears its name today. Notice they were not just sinners, but exceedingly. Wicked and sinners is the description. So four centuries or so after the Flood, wickedness was abounding at least in various pockets of humanity. Even 100 years after the Flood rebellion manifested itself at Babel. Water destroyed the Antediluvian world. Fire will later destroy the cities of the plain.

Genesis 13:14 "And the LORD said unto Abram, after that Lot was separated from him, Lift up now thine eyes, and look from the place where thou art northward, and southward, and eastward, and westward:"

Notice the pilcrow at the beginning of the Chapter in most King James Bibles. This indicates a new paragraph or thought in the Verse system. It allows us to have Verses, while still understanding paragraph divisions. The pilcrow is a small flag-like identifying marker. Its presence here shows a new paragraph or thought. Most theologians see this as significant. Now that Abram has finally divested himself from all of his family, God speaks to him of the Covenant in the Land of Promise.

God tells Abram to look in every direction. Abram allowed Lot to have his choice of the best of the land. God says all will be Abram's.

Genesis 13:15 "For all the land which thou seest, to thee will I give it, and to thy seed for ever."

God here speaks of Abram and his seed forever. I assume this Covenant is still in effect. Abram's seed has their names etched on the gates of the New Jerusalem. God has not forgotten Israel. Though we are spiritual Israel, God still has a place in His heart for natural Israel as well.

God is claiming ownership of the Land. Of course the entire earth is the LORD's, and the fullness thereof. And God is explaining to Abram that He is giving him this land. This is the purpose of the call from Ur. This is the seriousness of not losing Sarai to Pharaoh. The land will be Abram's and his seed in perpetuity.

Genesis 13:16 "And I will make thy seed as the dust of the earth: so that if a man can number the dust of the earth, then shall thy seed also be numbered."

An old, sterile man receives an abundant promise. If the famine was continuing, the entire area where Abram was, was to a large degree, dust. God is here saying that Abram's seed would be so numerous, it would be beyond numbering. Of course, numbers are considered to be infinite. But it seems to be referring to his seed being so numerous no one could undertake the numbering of them accurately through the generations of time. Abram's natural and spiritual seed throughout the millennia is indeed numberless.

Genesis 13:17 "Arise, walk through the land in the length of it and in the breadth of it; for I will give it unto thee."

Look was the command in Verse 14, now walk through the land of promise is the command here. At Abram's advanced age, with a large multitude of people and cattle, it would be a substantial undertaking to walk through the land. Or possibly he could go alone. The land, is a reiteration of the Abrahamic Covenant. It seems to be re-emphasized in parts throughout this portion of Scripture.

Genesis 13:18 "Then Abram removed his tent, and came and dwelt in the plain of Mamre, which is in Hebron, and built there an altar unto the LORD."

Lot goes toward Sodom, Abram toward Hebron. Abram builds an altar. Archaeology reveals the depravity of the Canaanites during this time period. It was not just relegated to Sodom and the cities of the plain. But it does seem to be worse there.

Abram builds yet another altar to Jehovah. Abram would be travelling south toward Hebron from Bethel. Bethel and Hebron were a few miles apart. Lot would be going SE about 60 miles toward Sodom from Bethel. This is the first mention of Mamre in Scripture, which means "strength" or "fatness." Mamre is mentioned some ten times in the Bible. This is the first of 73 mentions of Hebron in the Bible. Hebron means "association."

Hebron is nestled 3,050 feet above sea level, giving it a near ideal year-round climate. In January, lows average in the upper 30's, and in July, highs are in the mid 80's on average. It snows on occasion, just as in Jerusalem.

Chapter 14

IN CHAPTER 14 WE ARE ACQUAINTED with war, restoration, and Melchizedek.

Genesis 14:1 "And it came to pass in the days of Amraphel king of Shinar, Arioch king of Ellasar, Chedorlaomer king of Elam, and Tidal king of nations;"

In Hebrew literature, Amraphel tends to be equated with Nimrod. The traditional view is that it refers to Hammurabi, but this understanding has fallen into disfavor recently. I think Dr. Bill Cooper in his book, "The Authenticity of the Book of Genesis" makes a decisive case from a detailed study that Hammurabi, he of the famous Law Code, is in fact, Amraphel.

Cooper goes on to tell us that Arioch has left us several inscriptions, one of which mentions the holy tree of Eridu, correlating that to the tree of life. He then gives the translation of an inscription Arioch left on a pagan temple. He also mentioned who his father was.

Chedorlaomer, whose name identifies him as a servant of the moon god, is used likewise by Dr. Cooper to eviscerate the JEPD Wellhausen hypothesis. Nuances in the transliteration of his name from Elamite to Hebrew would have been unknown to a Hebrew scribe of the 6-5th Century BC era.

Concerning Tidal and the Kings, Dr. Cooper, on page 93 of his exhilarating book, speaks of an incredible archaeological discovery made in 1895, which contains each of these four kings' names. All four are seen interacting politically. So, Tidal was a historical figure. Dr. Cooper in an appendix, even has a letter written from Hammurabi to Chedorlaomer.

Genesis 14:2 "That these made war with Bera king of Sodom, and with Birsha king of Gomorrah, Shinab king of Admah, and Shemeber king of Zeboiim, and the king of Bela, which is Zoar."

Four more kings are here named, with a fifth unnamed. Lot would have been well acquainted with at least Bera. It is fascinating that not long after Lot pitches his tent toward Sodom, he is embroiled in war. The way of transgressors is hard. Sin brings punishment with it, though it rains on the just and the unjust alike. Ussher has the rebellion of Verse 4 occurring in 1913 BC, around seven years after Lot's separation with Abram.

In archaeology, Shinab's name appears in Akkadian tablets from Ur, but it is unclear if it is the same Shinab. Shemeber's name appears in the Mari tablets, but again it is not certain if it is the same king referred to. Of the remainder, we have no record as of yet from archaeology. The information from this paragraph once again comes from Dr. Cooper. I will repeat, please do yourself a favor and get all of his books. They are the most unique, informative books I personally have ever read. Chuck Missler is the only person I know of that comes close.

Genesis 14:3 "All these were joined together in the vale of Siddim, which is the salt sea."

It is unclear whether Verse 3 is referring back to only Verse 2, or is also inclusive of Verse 1 as well. It could be referring to the war that initially subjugated the cities of the plain. Or it could just be referencing the fact that the five kings of the plain were gathered together in the vale of Siddim. Whether there are two wars mentioned here or only one is a matter of some dispute.

The salt sea, another name for the Dead Sea, used to be a vale, and evidently very fertile. If this is referencing where the five kings' cities were located, it is conclusive that the Dead Sea is where these five cities used to be. If it is referring to the vale of Siddim as a meeting place, or a place of war, then it later became the Dead Sea, as one would infer from the judgment wrought in Genesis 19. Siddim means "field" or "plain."

Genesis 14:4 "Twelve years they served Chedorlaomer, and in the thirteenth year they rebelled."

Either Chedorlaomer was the leading figure of the confederacy found in Verse 1, or he marshalled the other kings with their forces to subjugate the five kings of the plain. If Ussher's chronology is correct, Sodom and their related confederacy was under servitude when Lot went toward them. The typologies are clear. It looked enticing to Lot, but it was in bondage, just as sin looks enticing but brings us into bondage. Sin, bondage, rebellion were the works of the flesh condition of these cities of the plain. Some would say even the number 13 mentioned here has an ominous connotation to the sinners of the plain.

Genesis 14:5 "And in the fourteenth year came Chedorlaomer, and the kings that were with him, and smote the Rephaims in Ashteroth Karnaim, and the Zuzims in Ham, and the Emims in Shaveh Kiriathaim,"

We are not told what type servitude is here intended, whether pecuniary, physical, or both. But once it was broken, Chedorlaomer came to reclaim it. And it is not specifically mentioned per se how this servitude had initially been established, unless it was a war mentioned in Verse 2.

Rephaims means "giants." Just as there were pre-Flood giants, so are there post-Flood giants, almost four-and-a-half centuries after the Flood. Ashteroth Karnaim means "Ashteroth of the two horns." If Ashteroth was indeed the wife of Nimrod, the two peaks could be speaking of Nimrod and Tammuz, horns being a euphemism for power in the ancient world. Ashteroth means "fertility," and she was worshipped among many cultures, especially the Phoenicians and NW Canaan. Ashteroth, along with Asherah and Anath, were 3 jealous rivals in mythology. The close association with Baal leads some (or many) to believe that Baal refers to Nimrod.

The Zuzims mean "roving creatures." We begin to see how the unified confederacy is picking off the isolated tribes of the land. Ham means "hot" or "sunburnt." So the Rephaims lost the battle to the four kings in Ashteroth Karnaim, and the Zuzims in Ham (probably one of a multitude of places named for Noah's son or someone named after him). Now we see the Emims defeated in Shaveh Kiriathaim. Emims means "terrors," and were a Moabite tribe according to some. With a name like that, it would be interesting to know what kind of people they were! Shaveh Kiriathaim means "plain of the double city." It is not readily identified.

Genesis 14:6 "And the Horites in their mount Seir, unto Elparan, which is by the wilderness."

Continuing with the carnage the four kings are wreaking, we have the Horites being defeated. This defeat extended from Mount Seir to Elparan. Horite means "cave dweller Might they have some connection to the fabulous Petra? An Egyptian inscription from 1380 BC seems to indicate this is the case. Seir means "hairy or shaggy." Many equate Elparan with Elpalet at the northern tip of the Gulf of Aqaba.

Genesis 14:7 "And they returned, and came to Enmishpat, which is Kadesh, and smote all the country of the Amalekites, and also the Amorites, that dwelt in Hazezontamar."

This is quite a campaign for these four kings, hundreds of miles from home. Provision and military cohesion would have been challenges. Enmishpat means "spring of judgment," and is located in southern Palestine. Hazezontamar means "dividing the date palm," and is quite likely Engedi in the desert of Israel.

Genesis 14:8 "And there went out the king of Sodom, and the king of Gomorrah, and the king of Admah, and the king of Zeboiim, and the king of Bela (the same is Zoar;) and they joined battle with them in the vale of Siddim;"

Now the true object of the four kings' rage comes into view, the five kings of the plain. They had destroyed any hope of help for these kings, and had also replenished their supply lines, especially if the famine was still in the land.

Sodom means "burning." Gomorrah means "submersion." Admah means "red earth." Zeboiim means "gazelles," giving an interesting look at the animal distribution of the land at that time, possibly. Bela means destruction. Zoar, which was another name for Bela, means "insignificance."

Vales were often used in the ancient world, and even in modern times, as places for battle. The Battle of Waterloo being one example of many.

Genesis 14:9 "With Chedorlaomer the king of Elam, and with Tidal king of nations, and Amraphel king of Shinar, and Arioch king of Ellasar; four kings with five."

This Mesopotamian confederacy joins battle with the five kings of the fertile region around the Jordan River. The five kings would have home field advantage, so to speak, with all of the benefits that go with that. Surely they must have been preparing for this battle after hearing of the carnage being doled out on neighboring tribes. While the four kings of Mesopotamia (Sumer area) could replenish weaponry from the vanquished foes, much of those items may have been quite unfamiliar to them, being different implements and the like (size, weight, type, etc.). So weaponry alone, besides food and water, would seem to be an advantage for the five kings.

Genesis 14:10 "And the vale of Siddim was full of slimepits; and the kings of Sodom and Gomorrah fled, and fell there; and they that remained fled to the mountain."

Mesopotamia was quite technologically advanced. Metallurgy and weaponry were quite possibly more superior than those found in the cities of the Plain. We get a look at what the topography of the vale of Siddim was before it became the Dead Sea. The slime pits, slime also being used for mortar at Babel, would have played some role in the battle. The directing of men and chariots could have been quite difficult. The term "full here" indicates the slimepits were ubiquitous.

The language seems to indicate that Bera and Birsha were slain in the battle as they fled. It is interesting that the cities were monarchies, which obviously did not stop the debauchery within the cities. The mountain mentioned here was probably either Mount Sodom or Mount Nebo, both in close proximity.

Genesis 14:11 "And they took all the goods of Sodom and Gomorrah, and all their victuals, and went their way."

The four kings invaded the cities of the plain after defeating them in battle, specifically spoiling Sodom and Gomorrah. This was possibly the practice with most or all of their vanquished foes. The term "all" used here, means they were leaving them destitute. Not only defeated militarily, but quite spoiled, in regards to goods. The price they paid to not give tribute to Chedorlaomer was astronomical. They ended up losing all, at least at this point. Whether any of the other ravages of war were inflicted on the defeated, we are not told. Notice they got supplies for their journey back.

Genesis 14:12 "And they took Lot, Abram's brother's son, who dwelt in Sodom, and his goods, and departed."

Haran's son Lot is taken captive by the four king confederacy. Notice Lot dwelt in Sodom, not its outskirts. We later find that Lot sat in the gate of Sodom, a position normally reserved for either city elders or the finest of capitalists. According to Verse 16, this abduction included his wife, daughters, and servants.

Genesis 14:13 "And there came one that had escaped, and told Abram the Hebrew; for he dwelt in the plain of Mamre the Amorite, brother of Eshcol, and brother of Aner: and these were confederate with Abram."

This is the first of 26 uses of the word "Hebrew" in Scripture. The plain of Mamre (strength or fatness; possibly some relation to a terebinth tree) is here mentioned. A famous tree and cultic shrine was there. Uniquely, the term "druid" comes from "tree worshipper." The groves were used in idolatrous worship. The plain of Mamre was located about 2 miles north of Hebron. Mamre was an Amorite. Amorite means "sayer" or "mountaineer," and is mentioned some 85+ times in Scripture. They appear throughout most of pre-exilic Old Testament history. Mamer is seen to be the brother of Eschol and Aner. Eschol is mentioned six times in the Bible, all in the Pentateuch. His name means "cluster," and the twelve spies would later cut down an enormous cluster of grapes from his self-named region. Aner is mentioned three times in Scripture, and may be the basis for a city named as belonging to Manasseh (1 Chronicles 6:70). Aner means "boy."

The escapee of conquest tells Abram that Lot and his goods have been taken captive. How he knew of the connection between Abram and Lot, or who the messenger was is not known. The fact that Mamre, Eschol, and Aner were confederate with Abram means they had at a minimum a mutual defense pact. When the four kings began to pillage the land, possibly they banded together for survival. It was not uncommon in that era for these types of alliances.

Genesis 14:14 "And when Abram heard that his brother was taken captive, he armed his trained servants, born in his own house, three hundred and eighteen, and pursued them unto Dan."

Brother means "close male relative," i.e. "nephew" in this instance. We begin to see the enormity of Abram's wealth. He had 318 trained men for war and protection, all born in his house. This means he did not purchase them, or conquer them. He goes after Lot to Dan.

The mention of Dan in this Verse has led many to assume that Moses was referring from the time of his writing in the 15th century BC, back to Abram's time in referencing Dan. And that Moses would have somehow known what portion of the Holy Land would be ascribed to Dan, though it was not allotted until the time of Joshua. Others say it is a scribal emendation of a later hand. They then use this logic to say if Dan was inserted from a hand that was not Moses', then great swaths of the Pentateuch may contain non-Mosaic materials as well. The answer could very well be that there was a city named Dan in the land at that time, and it had nothing to do with the tribe of Dan.

So Abram had a trained army, all from his household. And evidently the Amorites and their men went after this Mesopotamian invader force along with Abram's force. What Abram armed his servants with, we do not know, but swords and arrows were known at that time period. This indicates as well that Abram kept the armaments from his trained men, possibly to quell an uprising or rebellion, or to keep them from extortion and robbery of neighbors. Or, it could simply mean he gave them better weapons, weapons of war, and not everyday weapons for use and training.

Genesis 14:15 "And he divided himself against them, he and his servants, by night, and smote them, and pursued them unto Hobah, which is on the left hand of Damascus."

Abram would have been about 86 at the time of this battle. But he went forth to war anyway. Saving Lot was very important to him, and was made possible by this unnamed messenger who came to him with the tidings of Lot's captivity.

The battle plan aligns closely with Gideon's. Dividing his army, probably surrounding them, he gave the appearance of a much larger force. He engaged the battle at night for maximum surprise and confusion. And Abram's army won. We have no way of knowing how large the Mesopotamian army was, but it is generally thought, due to its epic line of victories, that it was quite large.

Dan, whether a city then existing or a reference to future Dan, was in the north of Israel. Hobah means "hiding place," and was east and possibly north of Damascus, or a little over 150 miles from Abram's starting point in the plain of Mamre. Abram shows himself to be a brave warrior, which is an OT theme, with Moses, David, and Joshua being warriors as well. As long as they were right with God, they never lost a battle.

Also, we are not sure if Abram devised the battle plan, or if it was Divinely directed by God.

Genesis 14:16 "And he brought back all the goods, and also brought again his brother Lot, and his goods, and the women also, and the people."

Abram was careful in battle to only slay the enemy. He recovered all of the goods that had been taken. The use of the term "smote" in Verse 15 indicates injuring and slaying the enemy. The term "slaughter" is used in Verse 17. It is not known the totality of the casualties on the Mesopotamian side. There must have been some irony as well, as the four kings Abram was facing were from close proximity of Ur his native land.

Genesis 14:17 "And the king of Sodom went out to meet him after his return from the slaughter of Chedorlaomer, and of the kings that were with him, at the valley of Shaveh, which is the king's dale."

The king of Sodom was taken captive, as were the other kings of the plain of Jordan. Verse 10 indicates strongly that Bera and Birsha were killed, so this must be referring to their replacements. Shaveh is located just north of Jerusalem. Shaveh means "plain" or "level plain." Dale means "valley" or "open country."

Sodom's prominence in the five cities of the plain arrangement is apparent. We find in Verse 21 he just wanted his people back, not their substance. This may give some insight into his mind and motives.

Genesis 14:18 "And Melchizedek king of Salem brought forth bread and wine: and he was the priest of the most high God."

We are here introduced to one of the most mysterious yet prominent characters in the Bible, Melchizedek. His name means "king of righteousness" (Melchi – king; zedek – righteousness). Salem means "peace," and is where we get the modern term, "Shalom." Salem became known as Jerusalem. Melchizedek is mentioned with this spelling twice in the Bible here, and in Psalm 110:4. In the Book of Hebrews he is mentioned nine times in Chapters 5-7, with his name spelled "Melchisedec." The most-high God is "El Elyon" in Hebrew. This is the first of 53 uses of the Hebrew word in the Bible, five times in Genesis and nine times in the Pentateuch.

Melchizedek was king of Salem and a priest of the most-high God. Many Hebrews identify him with Shem, who would have still been alive at this point. Others, based primarily on the Passages in Hebrews, liken Melchizedek to a Theophany (a visible manifestation of God in the OT), the Word, Jehovah, a Christophany, or something representing the Divine, if not the Divine Himself. In the 19 words of this Verse, we find he is king in Salem. Of course Jerusalem, which is Salem, Salem just being an early form or abbreviated, is the city of the great King, God (Psalm 48:2). Bringing bread and wine certainly seems typological of communion. And being a priest, again the typology of Jesus is definitely noticeable, as Jesus was a King/Priest, who shall rule and reign in Jerusalem.

Melchizedek's Kingdom seems to have been untouched by the marauding Mesopotamian forces. This could be by Divine Favor, or the fact that Jerusalem is surrounded by mountains at a very high elevation (2200 feet plus). In Hebrews we read He had an everlasting priesthood, and at the very least is a type of Jesus.

Genesis 14:19 "And he blessed him, and said, Blessed be Abram of the most high God, possessor of heaven and earth:"

The less is blessed of the better according to Hebrews 7:7. So, for Melchizedek to be the one doing the blessing is certainly amazing, considering the object of his blessing, Abram. In Abram all the world would be blessed, but Melchizedek was greater. We also see the blessing as a theme in Genesis. God blesses creation in Chapter 1, and

Noah and his family after the Flood. The blessing will play a vital role in the remainder of the Patriarchal period, and indeed throughout the remainder of Scripture. There is definitely power in blessing.

We get to see the words spoken in this blessing in Verses 19 and 20. He spoke 28 words of blessing in all. He begins by acknowledging God's Highness and Supremacy. He is the Almighty, as God will identify Himself in Genesis 17:1, and will be used in reference to Jesus in Revelation 1:8. Jesus is the Almighty God, the Father and the Son in one Person.

Notice next Melchizedek goes into God being the possessor of heaven and earth. God is not only the Creator, He is the Owner. The earth is the Lord's and the fulness therof.

Genesis 14:20 "And blessed be the most high God, which hath delivered thine enemies into thy hand. And he gave him tithes of all."

We now see God is blessed. He is the Fount, Origination, and Power behind all blessing. He is the very definition of Blessing. Jesus is called "God blessed forever" in Romans 9:5. We see this thanksgiving that Abram's enemies are delivered into his hand. Abram's seed would even possess the gate of his enemies. The Church is Abram's seed, and the gates of hell cannot prevail against it.

Though the text is seemingly ambiguous, it is clear from the context that Abram gave Melchizedek tithes, or ten percent of everything. We are not sure what happened to the four kings of the east, or their goods. But there is a chance this was an enormous amount of goods. This is the first mention of tithes in the Bible, but it is evident that it was known, just as the difference of unclean and clean animals was known. Tithing was before, during, and after the law, and Jesus said tithing even the smallest things was good. The tithe belongs to the LORD. We will find Jacob tithing, or pledging to, later in Genesis.

Notice the end of the blessing. Though Abram and his servants had gone out to win the war, it was God who did the delivering. We can pray, but it is God Who does the answering. We can work, but it is God which does the blessing.

Genesis 14:21 "And the king of Sodom said unto Abram, Give me the persons, and take the goods to thyself."

The pilcrow at the beginning of this Verse and the next show differences of thought, what we may call paragraphs. Though Bera or his successor had been vanquished, they were still king. God raises up leaders, the powers that be are ordained of God. The king of Sodom probably thought he was being humble, only asking for the people and not the goods. But he may have been bold as well. He may have suspected that Abram, due to his victory, would keep his people, so he decided to ask for them back. Notice as well that even though his army had been defeated, they were still following him. Rebellion didn't seem to be much of an option.

Genesis 14:22 "And Abram said to the king of Sodom, I have lift up mine hand unto the LORD, the most high God, the possessor of heaven and earth,"

We still lift up our hand when we make an oath before God, such as at a trial. We notice also that Abram uses the same phraseology to describe God as Melchizedek. Possibly Abram's encounter with Melchizedek had made quite the impression on him. So, Abram gives Melchizedek tithes from the spoil. The wealth of the sinner is laid up for the just. Lifting of hands, whether in Moses' time, or in the Church (1 Timothy 2:8) is a Biblical principle.

Abram gave to Melchizedek, and he will give much back to the king of Sodom. Abram had rescued Lot and his family, that was enough.

Genesis 14:23 "That I will not take from a thread even to a shoelatchet, and that I will not take any thing that is thine, lest thou shouldest say, I have made Abram rich:"

Abram refuses to take even partial articles, such as a thread or a shoe latchet from Sodom. Concerning the shoe latchet, Ootsi the Ice Man, the near perfectly preserved ancient man found frozen in

Europe, probably at least 4,000 years old, had incredibly designed clothing, including shoes. The use of a shoe latchet in the advanced civilizations of the ANE should not be surprising. They could build the Great Pyramid and the Sphinx, after all.

We see that Abram acknowledges the possessions of the king of Sodom. And he wanted to give all glory to God. It was God the possessor of heaven and earth that had blessed Abram and made him rich, not the king of Sodom. The king of Sodom was probably the king of the confederacy, and represented them all. There is a chance, however, that he was the only one of the five kings that came to retrieve his people. He got his possessions, as well.

Genesis 14:24 "Save only that which the young men have eaten, and the portion of the men which went with me, Aner, Eshcol, and Mamre; let them take their portion."

Abram continues his dialogue with the king of Sodom. You'll notice in Verse 23 the use of the words, "thine" and "thou," singular words, showing he is speaking to the king of Sodom only. Abram here begins to list his conditions, that he would return the people, and all of the goods with two exceptions: Replenishing what the young men had eaten, and what Aner, Eschol, and Mamre would deem necessary. It is not entirely clear if it is only what they and any troops they supplied had eaten, or other goods were involved, as well. Lot is safe, for now. Abram is victorious. And the replenishing of the food may indicate the famine was still at least somewhat in the Land.

Chapter 15

CHAPTER 15 IS ONE OF THE PIVOTAL Passages in the Bible. We see a dramatic cutting of the Covenant with God and Abram, and then an extended dialogue of God and Abram. Let's begin.

Genesis 15:1 "After these things the word of the LORD came unto Abram in a vision, saying, Fear not, Abram: I am thy shield, and thy exceeding great reward."

Ussher keeps this event at 1911 BC. After the battle, the word of the LORD comes to Abram in a vision. When Jesus comes back, His Name is called the Word of God (Revelation 19:13). Of course, He is the Word of John 1:1. So many would equate this with not merely a spoken word by Jehovah, but with God Himself. Can you separate a person from their word? Some would say that this is the Visible of the Invisible, the Utterance of the Divine Mind. Each instance of the word of the LORD coming and speaking should be taken in isolation. It doesn't always seem to represent the Person of Jehovah Himself in a personified form, but in many cases it does.

God's Word to Abram was to "fear not" initially. It is interesting the number of times that even angels seem to cause fear on even the holiest, such as Isaiah's unworthiness, and on John and Daniel. Now it also does not say Abram was asleep here. Many people think a vision is a dream when you are awake. That could very well be what is happening here.

After the battle, God announces that He is Abram's shield. After paying tithes, and refusing to take the goods of Sodom and company, God announces He is Abram's great reward. The king of Sodom cannot take credit for making Abram rich, only God can. A nomadic traveler getting blessed along the way, even in Egypt. This promise from God would serve Abram well the rest of his life.

Genesis 15:2 "And Abram said, Lord GOD, what wilt thou give me, seeing I go childless, and the steward of my house is this Eliezer of Damascus?"

In ancient laws and contracts discovered in the ANE, it was quite common and customary for the steward to become the heir of a childless marriage. Eliezer will play a prominent role in Chapter 24, if indeed it is the same person.

Abram seems to be saying if my seed is going to bless the world, will it come through Eliezer? How Eliezer came to work with Abram we are not told. Jehovah Elohim is once again used by Abram to address God. Abram at this time was about 85, making his battle victory of the previous Chapter the more impressive.

Genesis 15:3 "And Abram said, Behold, to me thou hast given no seed: and, lo, one born in my house is mine heir."

Abram acknowledged that it is God that gives the seed, that gives life into the world. He is reminding God of the fact that under current circumstances, Eliezer was his heir. It is also interesting to note that Abram at 85 had not yet lived half his life. He had already done so much. But both in the Scriptural account, and in age, he was just getting started, so to speak. That seems to be a theme in the Pentateuch. Noah seems to have really begun his ministry at 500. Moses was 80 and Aaron 83 when they lead the Exodus. Was it Allan Oggs' father who was in his 60's when he was called to preach? I can't remember for sure, but what I can assure you of is while you have breath in your body, do all you can for Jesus. The best may occur in the latter part of your life. James Kilgore was in his 80's teaching Bible College in the Philippines and soul winning young Americans at Starbucks.

Genesis 15:4 "And, behold, the word of the LORD came unto him, saying, This shall not be thine heir; but he that shall come forth out of thine own bowels shall be thine heir."

In this open vision, the word of the LORD possibly has what some have called a Spirit Body. Or it could just have God putting the words from Him into Abram's mind. Regardless, God emphatically informs Abram that Eliezer was not the heir, but that Abram was still going to give birth from his own seed. But since Sarai was not mentioned here, possibly they misunderstood, and this will lead to the Hagar and Ishmael episode of Chapter 16. Notice the "he" comes from Abram's bowels, a very strongly pro-life statement.

Genesis 15:5 "And he brought him forth abroad, and said, Look now toward heaven, and tell the stars, if thou be able to number them: and he said unto him, So shall thy seed be."

The word of the LORD is God Himself, not a separate person. So the word brings Abram forth. Without light pollution, Abram quite probably could see the Milky Way. So this event is happening at night. Someone counted 7,000 plus stars available to the naked eye in optimal conditions. But with the Milky Way, the number would have been innumerable to count. Always remember the sky is full of stars, but you just can't see them when the sun is shining. And the sun shines in the day, you can't see it when it's cloudy, but it is still there. Spiritual lessons abound about Jesus the Sun of righteousness.

Now you could make the argument that it was daylight here, and God was saying since you can't see the stars, so your seed will be uncountable. And the only star you see is the sun, which represents Messiah, which will outshine all of your other seed. Maybe that is the interpretation, but you certainly couldn't say that conclusively. Verse 12 may be further corroboration, however. But it could have just as well been at night. The point stands either way. Abram's seed would be innumerable even though he was currently childless.

In Revelation 12 stars represent angels. Here they represent the seed of Abram. My 'ole Pastor used to say that the stars represented Abram's spiritual seed, and the sand represented his natural seed, Israel. Where God brought Abram abroad, we do not know, and we are not sure if it was a spiritual carrying or a natural leading.

Genesis 15:6 "And he believed in the LORD; and he counted it to him for righteousness."

In this very significant Chapter is found one of the most pivotal Verses in all of the Bible. Romans 4, Galatians 3, and James 2 all refer back to this Passage. "In" is a preposition. Karl Barth said in Romans for example, the key to understanding the Book is understanding the prepositions. Abram had seemingly believed God before. He believed Him enough to come out of Ur to a land he knew not of (Hebrews 11:8 reads, "By faith Abraham, when he was called to go out into a place which he should after receive for an inheritance, obeyed; and he went out, not knowing whither he went."). But uniquely Abram according to this context of Chapter 15, believed God for a child, a seed. And not just for a child, but that the child would have copious progeny. And because Abram believed that, God counted it to him for righteousness. Abram was a sinner. But God said if you will believe this enormous promise, I count it to you for righteousness. Righteousness is found 306 times in Scripture. In this particular context, it means to account pure or right. Abram's belief in the great promise of God brought a right standing with God to him. Our belief in One of Abram's Seed, Jesus, brings righteousness to us.

Believing "in" the LORD, and not "of" or "on," or some other preposition could be quite significant. While one or more of the prepositions may be synonymous, in seems here to be very particularly chosen. In could very well mean Jehovah's Character and Nature, His Essence and essential Being. Abram did not just believe this particular promise, but everything about Jehovah. The assurance of His Word, and His ability to bring it to pass. "Counted" is another significant Word, as I guess they all are in Holy Writ. God had just had Abram to count the stars if he could. Now He counts (awards or rewards) this to Abram as righteousness. Abram could not work his way into this proposition. At a certain visceral, deep level, He had to believe it absolutely. It entered the warp and woof of Abram's being.

Notice the sovereignty and free-will aspect here as well. God sovereignly developed the plan. Yet Abram by his choice had to believe the plan.

Genesis 15:7 "And he said unto him, I am the LORD that brought thee out of Ur of the Chaldees, to give thee this land to inherit it."

Abraham had to leave Ur by faith (Hebrews 11:8), but it was God who had brought him out. Jehovah was a Name that was used, but the full Covenantal import of the Name was not yet fully known (Exodus 6:3). God's promises were constantly to Abram and His Seed (Messiah). I will give you the land. I will give you a seed. I will give a multitude of descendants.

We probably should give more attention to the word "seed." While seed can either be singular or plural, Paul makes a big deal of seed being singular with respect to Abraham (Galatians 3:16, one of the many great 3:16's in Scripture). Comparing Verses 5 and 6 here in Chapter 15, it could very well mean that Abram understood that Jehovah would be the seed, i.e. that Jehovah would be born of the seed of Abraham in the future (Hebrews 2:16). And Jesus' body would be the Church, mentioned as a body over 30 times in Scripture, hence the stars.

"Inherit" would mean that it would be to Abram's descendants. And it was Jehovah that watched over Abram to bring him out of Ur, to bring him into his land of promise. God made the promise and plan, and Abram obeyed.

Genesis 15:8 "And he said, Lord GOD, whereby shall I know that I shall inherit it?"

Abram believed in the LORD. He believed wholeheartedly in Him.

But he desired a sign. Adonai Elohim, I want to know that I will inherit it. He believed that his seed would be numerous. Now he wants to know how he can be assured the land will be his perpetuity. It is fascinating that like Moses, Abram talks to God face to face, so to speak.

Genesis 15:9 "And he said unto him, Take me an heifer of three years old, and a she goat of three years old, and a ram of three years old, and a turtledove, and a young pigeon."

The root word for covenant is "berit" in Hebrew, and indicates a cutting, and the concomitant shedding of blood. God here tells Abram to take five animals: two females, a male ram, and two birds. Harold Sheppard of Columbus Georgia preached years ago about these animals representing the five-fold ministry. I am sure each of the animals has a special significance. It is beyond the scope of this study to explore what that is. But much like the Law of Moses, and Noah's sacrifice, Abel's, and the coat of skins in the Garden, these sacrifices would be significant as well. Blood must be shed in the covenant. Death for life.

Genesis 15:10 And he took unto him all these, and divided them in the midst, and laid each piece one against another: but the birds divided he not."

So the three mammals of livestock he cut in half, but not the two fowls. The confirmation of the covenant is unfolding. Abram had asked for assurance for inheriting the land. He was about to receive that in this cutting of the covenant with God. Abram was assured about his seed, but not the land.

Genesis 15:11 "And when the fowls came down upon the carcases, Abram drove them away."

Obviously dead carcasses are going to attract predators, in this case, fowls. We are still not informed where this is taking place, only that

God had brought Abram forth abroad. Wouldn't it be amazing if this scene was on Mt. Calvary? The fowls mentioned here are not the two mentioned in Verse 10, at least that is the assumption. It has not yet officially stated the two fowl of Verses 9 and 10 were killed, but that is assumed. Abram must have known the animals were significant, to drive away the fowls, like Rizpah would do almost a millennia later with her deceased sons.

Genesis 15:12 "And when the sun was going down, a deep sleep fell upon Abram; and, lo, an horror of great darkness fell upon him."

Intense darkness fell on Egypt in the ninth plague, and again will fall on the world in the Great Tribulation in the Wrath of God. We find the time was evening, dusk. Just as a deep sleep came on Adam in Genesis 2:21, a deep sleep comes on Abram here. Psalm 127:2 says, "… he giveth his beloved sleep."

A horror of great darkness falls upon Abram. Pitch black terror. Possibly a darkness that could be felt. It would be difficult to tell exactly how this felt, but the description is full of intensity. A few Scriptures for Context before we go to God speaking in Verse 13 is in order.

"And he made darkness pavilions round about him, dark waters, and thick clouds of the skies." 2 Samuel 22:12

"He made darkness his secret place; his pavilion round about him were dark waters and thick clouds of the skies." Psalm 18:11

Also, if the stars episode of Verse 5 was at night, the contrast is here noticed. Promise or terror.

Genesis 15:13 "And he said unto Abram, Know of a surety that thy seed shall be a stranger in a land that is not theirs, and shall serve them; and they shall afflict them four hundred years;"

God begins to tell Abram the future with great specificity. This is one of several times God speaks to Abram. No wonder he is called a friend of God.

God begins by telling Abram to know something for sure; that his yet unborn but promised seed would be a stranger in a land that was not theirs. He did not mention Egypt at this time. Many would say that Egypt's rule extended into Canaan at this time. God also tells Abram that not only would his seed be a stranger in a land not belonging to them, but that his seed would serve this land. And the service would be with affliction, or torment. Ussher would put this Chapter around 1912(11) BC. The 400 years would begin when Ishmael, from the Egyptian Hagar, mocked Isaac in 1891 BC when Isaac was five years old. This would put the Exodus at 1491 BC. I understand that current dating methods put rather conclusively in conservative scholarship the Exodus at 1446 BC. I have yet to see where Ussher is wrong, but I do stand to be corrected. I may go into further detail of why the 1446 BC date has gained prominence at another time. Reese and Floyd Nolen Jones are two powerful witnesses maintaining the 1491 BC date for the Exodus. In the Book of Exodus, we will be confronted with a 430 year time period, which seems to coincide with Abram's departure from Haran earlier in Genesis.

The specificness of which God speaks is verifiable. God pronounces prophecies as a matter of His Godhood. See Isaiah among dozens of other references.

Genesis 15:14 "And also that nation, whom they shall serve, will I judge: and afterward shall they come out with great substance."

The fulfillment of this in the Exodus is beyond dispute. When studying Exodus, it is beneficial to look at this Verse for background. God is judging Egypt, as well as delivering His people. He judges the gods of Egypt according to Scripture.

Genesis 15:15 "And thou shalt go to thy fathers in peace; thou shalt be buried in a good old age."

God goes from Abram's seed and descendants, to Abram's life. Abram had just been in an epic battle, quite possibly enormously outnumbered. But God tells Abram that his final end will be in peace, not war. And that Abram, even at his advanced age, will live to a good old age. Also, he will not be abandoned, or burnt, but rather buried. Cremation in Scripture is a pagan practice. Burying was the practice among God's people. Look at Jesus.

Genesis 15:16 "But in the fourth generation they shall come hither again: for the iniquity of the Amorites is not yet full."

We learn from this Verse that a generation in Abram's time was 100 years. Abram lived to be 175 years old, or 105 years past the threescore and ten of current lifespans. Most say a current generation is 40 years.

God's foreknowledge is perfect. He knew the Amorites would continue to sin. But in His justice, there is a time of His choosing for His judgements. God is longsuffering and merciful. He waits until His Holiness is violated to the point it tips the scales in judgment.

According to Genesis 14:13, Abram dwelt in the plain of Mamre the Amorite. It is quite possible he was personally acquainted with their (the Amorites) wickedness.

Genesis 15:17 "And it came to pass, that, when the sun went down, and it was dark, behold a smoking furnace, and a burning lamp that passed between those pieces."

God has been speaking to Abram while a deep sleep and a horror of great darkness was upon him. It is not known whether Abram was awakened by God's Voice, or whether God was speaking to him while he was asleep. It is not entirely clear if Abram is here awake and seeing this come to pass, or he is still asleep. It is fascinating that while Adam was asleep, God made a covenant partner with him in Eve. While Abram is asleep, God is making a covenant with him.

The smoking furnace and burning lamp are generally thought to represent God, though it doesn't specifically mention that here. But the passing through of halved animals does seem to be a practice of covenants in the ANE.

Jesus, our Lamb, was bleeding, striped, pierced, and between heaven and earth while He was making the New Covenant with man.

The veil of the Temple, and His Flesh, was torn, revealing the Glory of God. Certain similarities and shadows to the events mentioned here.

Genesis 15:18 "In the same day the LORD made a covenant with Abram, saying, Unto thy seed have I given this land, from the river of Egypt unto the great river, the river Euphrates:"

Jehovah makes a covenant with Abram. The land was going to belong to Abram's seed. God deeded it to him. This also lets us see that God honors private property. The extent of the covenant is far greater than the Dan to Beersheba found later, and is larger than the inheritance proffered in Joshua. The closest Israel has ever yet gotten to this fulfillment is during the time of Solomon. The River of Egypt is sometimes thought to be the Nile, but others feel a smaller river north and east of the Nile is meant.

The land area promised by God to Abram's yet unborn seed is nearly the entire area of his lifetime of travel, from North and West of Ur, all the way to his journey into Egypt, at least partially.

Genesis 15:19 "The Kenites, and the Kenizzites, and the Kadmonites,"

God, in the next three Verses, details 10 tribes or people groups that He will give to Abram's seed. It is possible that earlier the Amorites were a euphemism for the entirety of these 10 tribes, being possibly the largest or earliest established.

Kenites mean "smiths." They are recognizable as Jethro's lineage. Many think they inhabited somewhere on either side of the Gulf of Aquba.

The Kenizzites are descendants of Kenaz. Kenaz is listed as a descendant of Esau, but it is not clear if that is the same as is meant here. The Kadmonites mean "easterners." It is assumed this means around the Dead Sea region, but little if anything is currently definitively known of them.

Genesis 15:20 "And the Hittites, and the Perizzites, and the Rephaims,"

Three more people groups are mentioned here. The Hittites were a predominate people in the ANE. When their capital Boghazkoy was discovered, it was monumental in validating Scripture, as in the 19th century AD they were considered by liberal scholars to be mythological and non-existent. The Hittites are mentioned throughout the Old Testament, with perhaps the most famous being Uriah the Hittite, husband of Bathsheba.

The Perizzites, which means "belonging to a village," seem to have eventually dwelled in the plains and mountains of Canaan. The Rephaims mean "giants." Giants seem to have been rather prominent in the Holy Land. Perizzites are mentioned 23 times in Scripture, beginning in Genesis 13. Rephaim(s) are mentioned eight times, beginning in Chapter 14.

Genesis 15:21 "And the Amorites, and the Canaanites, and the Girgashites, and the Jebusites."

Four more tribes are here mentioned as given to the seed of Abram. Amorite(s) are found 86 times in Scripture, making them a leading non-Israelite people group in the Old Testament. Canaanites or Canaan is found 157 times throughout the Bible. Canaan means "lowland," and the Promised Land is sometimes referred to as "Canaan." This area is sometimes also generally referred to as the Levant. The Girgashites are found six times in Scripture, and their name means "dwelling in clayey soil." The Jebusites are basically the dwellers in and around Jerusalem, which in Chapter 14 was known as Salem. They are found 41 times in Holy Writ, beginning in Chapter 10. Their name means "descendants of Jebus." Jebus was a name for at least part of Jerusalem for a millennia, or so it seems.

Genesis 16

Genesis 16:1 "Now Sarai Abram's wife bare him no children: and she had an handmaid, an Egyptian, whose name was Hagar."

We are now introduced to Hagar, who is mentioned 12 times in Scripture. Her name means "flight." It is deduced by most that she was part of the spoil given by Pharaoh to Abram for Sarai. That is by no means certain, however. Sarai, being the wife of an extremely wealthy individual, would have had assistance. Hagar was a handmaid, a servant. We are not sure of the number of servants that Sarai had to assist her. In laws of the time, discovered in archaeology, it was allowable, and even customary for a barren wife to give her handmaid to her husband to bear a child. Most times the child would be considered the Mistress's of the house. This surrogacy was not unusual at that time and culture.

Genesis 16:2 "And Sarai said unto Abram, Behold now, the LORD hath restrained me from bearing: I pray thee, go in unto my maid; it may be that I may obtain children by her. And Abram hearkened to the voice of Sarai."

Abram had been assured of a seed. In 15:2, he had thought that possibly his steward, Eliezar of Damascus would be the heir. In 15:4, God assures Abram that the seed would come from his own loins. Quite possibly Abram thought this may be the fulfillment.

In the New Covenant, we have a higher standard. A better covenant established upon better promises. God at one time winked at certain things, but now due to the New Birth, expects more of His children. Practices such as this and polygamy, and conquest by physical war, are no longer part of God's New Covenant plan.

The theme of the man listening to the voice of the woman is again brought to the fore. God had just had a lengthy conversation with Abram. But Abram listens to Sarai's voice. This will be seen as a theme of Genesis, and other parts of Scripture. Even in Proverbs, the typology of the woman's voice, with a secondary application referring to false religion, will be seen. Look at Solomon.

Sarai said it was Jehovah who had restrained her from bearing. Without a lengthy discourse, we cannot go into all of the different views on that. Typology certainly played a part. The birthing difficulties of Abram's descendants will be a topic throughout the remainder of Genesis.

We see as well Abram was not permitted to assume the taking of Hagar for child bearing without the consent of his wife. This is also seen in ANE law codes in many instances.

Genesis 16:3 "And Sarai Abram's wife took Hagar her maid the Egyptian, after Abram had dwelt ten years in the land of Canaan, and gave her to her husband Abram to be his wife."

This very well could have been an official ceremony. I'm not sure if Hagar could have refused or not. In that culture, which was more socially advanced at times than is generally thought, it would have probably not been a viable decision for Hagar to refuse.

Abram is here about 85 years of age. We are not sure of Hagar's age. Hagar was not just to be a surrogate, but a wife. She was being promoted from being a handmaid, to a wife. Now she would not have equal rights with Sarai. But she would have more rights than a regular handmaid. This would have been about 1911 BC. Arphaxad, Noah's grandson, would not die until three years later, in 1908 BC.

Genesis 16:4 "And he went in unto Hagar, and she conceived: and when she saw that she had conceived, her mistress was despised in her eyes."

Hagar conceived. And as is natural, at least in some females, she began to be possessive of Abram. Sarai was despised by Hagar. She had gone from servant to wife, to bearer of a firstborn of one of the richest men in the Country, and possibly one of the richest men in the world. She was probably quite a bit younger than Sarai, who would have been 75 at this time. She had gone from having basically nothing, to having the possibility of great wealth. She also knew, if by some fluke, Sarai was to have a child, it would relegate her seed to second place, just in order of hierarchy. So this confluence of emotions came on Hagar. And she despised Sarai. This possibly meant she quit taking orders from Sarai for service.

Genesis 16:5 "And Sarai said unto Abram, My wrong be upon thee: I have given my maid into thy bosom; and when she saw that she had conceived, I was despised in her eyes: the LORD judge between me and thee."

I love this. Sarai says, my wrong be upon thee. She did not take personal responsibility for concocting the plan. Or at least the results of it. She did admit she did wrong. But the consequences would be on Abram. It reminds me of a Garden when another man listened to his wife. This is not to say that men should not give heed to their wives' opinions and thoughts. They should. But they should always take God's Word and plan over anyone else's, including their wife's.

Sarai goes on to say Jehovah is going to have to judge between Abram's choice and Sarai. In the pre-New Covenant world, where the sinful nature had no pushback from a New Birth experience, it was, to say the least, an interesting time. For a wife to give probably a much younger woman to be with their devoted husband, would probably be quite a shock for the first wife. Sarai had been a great wife. She had willingly gone with Abram through all his journeys, even in advanced age. But marital and home harmony had been violated. There was now a problem.

My Pastor used to say, don't birth an Ishmael. Ishmael is what we get when we don't wait for God's plan. Ishmael was still blessed, but he wasn't the seed of promise. And there is conflict to this day between Ishmael's seed and Isaac's seed. The flesh and the Spirit, as Paul points out so poignantly in Galatians 4.

Genesis 16:6 "But Abram said unto Sarai, Behold, thy maid is in thy hand; do to her as it pleaseth thee. And when Sarai dealt hardly with her, she fled from her face."

Abram doesn't acknowledge Hagar as his wife, but as Sarai's maid. Notice Abram says her maid is in her hand. Abram gave her free reign to do whatever was needed to rectify the situation. He trusted Sarai, and gave her full control over the situation. But you could also say, his reasoning might have been, you got us into this mess, you get us out.

In Verse 5 we see that Sarai comes to Abram for resolution. My wrong be upon thee, Abram. But Abram flips the narrative. You deal with her.

In this battle of the women, the conflict of Abram's wives, Sarai had the upper hand. She was backed by the entire household. Hagar, a servant girl, with rampant emotions, was alone. And Sarai decided to break Hagar, so to speak. But maybe it was necessary in the situation. But Sarai dealt hardly, or harshly with Hagar. But Hagar would not submit. In her emotional state, she fled from Sarai. It will become obvious that whatever plan she had when she fled, did not have much chance of working. She was pregnant after all, only compounding the difficulties of being alone in a dangerous land.

Sarai was wrong for the offer. Abram was wrong for accepting. Jacob was offered two handmaidens from his wives. What one generation does in moderation, a later will do in excess. This will be seen in the Patriarchal time. And Hagar was wrong for a bad attitude, and a refusal to submit to her mistress. Two or three wrongs have never yet equaled one right.

Genesis 16:7 "And the angel of the LORD found her by a fountain of water in the wilderness, by the fountain in the way to Shur."

The angel of the LORD is thought by some to be a specific angel, or even a Theophany or Christophany. The modifier "the" is thought by many to differentiate this angel from other angels. Others would just identify this as the angel specific to dealing with Hagar in this Passage. A few Scriptures to consider may be in order.

Exodus 23:20, 21 "Behold, I send an Angel before thee, to keep thee in the way, and to bring thee into the place which I have prepared." "Beware of him, and obey his voice, provoke him not; for he will not pardon your transgressions: for my name is in him." So an angel invested with God's Name.

Isaiah 63:9 "In all their affliction he was afflicted, and the angel of his presence saved them: in his love and in his pity he redeemed them; and he bare them, and carried them all the days of old." And an angel invested with God's Presence.

Some go so far as to say that this particular angel is a Theophany (Visible Presence or manifestation of God, without a fleshly body), and the term the angel of the LORD is not found in the NT because it is fulfilled in Christ. However, Matthew 1:20, 24; Matthew 2:13, 28:2; Luke 2:9, and at least four times in Acts all mention the angel of the Lord. Of course, the all caps is missing, because that is basically an Old Testament convention representing the Tetragrammaton, or Jehovah (YHWH). Tetragrammaton merely means "the four letters."

Shur means "wall," and is generally thought to be either in extreme NE Egypt, or SW Palestine. The general picture is that Hagar was going back to Egypt. Whether two fountains are here meant in the Verse, or one referred to twice, is somewhat unclear. It seems to me to be referring to one well. Hagar being in the wilderness going to Egypt may have some echoes of symbolism with Israel in the wilderness coming out of Egypt some 400 years or so later.

Hagar is by a fountain in a fairly dry area. She is Abram's wife. She has his seed, though it is not his promised seed. God has not forgotten this Egyptian woman full of emotion. God had obviously sent the angel. Some would also possibly identify this angel as one of the Seven Spirits of God.

Genesis 16:8 "And he said, Hagar, Sarai's maid, whence camest thou? and whither wilt thou go? And she said, I flee from the face of my mistress Sarai."

As we have seen also with God in Genesis, this angel is prone to ask questions. This seems to be a device used by Holy Beings to make us think and confront ourselves. Parents still do this to children. Did you grab the cookie jar, did you hit your sibling, and the like, knowing full well they did.

Notice that the angel refers to Hagar by her name, and then identifies her as Sarai's maid and not Abram's wife. The angel knew it was out of God's order. According to Galatians 4 Hagar represented the flesh.

The angel, not being omniscient, may not have known where Hagar had come from. Maybe he was on assignment from God, and did not have that detail. And not being omniscient, he also did not know where she was going. Or it could be he was trying to get Hagar to answer the questions. Hagar answered both questions in nine words. She fled from the face of her mistress Sarai. Maybe Sarai's face had been ablaze in anger and harsh words when she dealt hardly with Hagar. Again we see that Hagar seemingly had no definitive plan per se where she was going. She was just fleeing from her mistress. Possibly she was going back to Egypt.

It is fascinating to me that even Hagar acknowledged that Sarai was still her mistress, or the one that Hagar served. She was Abram's wife, but still subordinate.

Genesis 16:9 "And the angel of the LORD said unto her, Return to thy mistress, and submit thyself under her hands."

Hagar had despised Sarai. She was not in an attitude of submission. Proverbs 13:10 says that only by pride cometh contention. But now the angel of God says to go and return to Sarai her mistress, and submit to whatever harshness Sarai would give. The human element of Scripture is not to be missed. What the angel was asking her to do was not easy in the complex situation Hagar was in.

I have often said, if we will read the Bible with our children, we will never have to explain the birds and the bees to them. The Scripture has more drama than soap operas do many times. This is one of those times filled with pathos.

Genesis 16:10 "And the angel of the LORD said unto her, I will multiply thy seed exceedingly, that it shall not be numbered for multitude."

The angel here begins to speak as God. The angel did not have power to increase Hagar's seed, but God does. Some, of course, would say the angel speaks that way because it really is God as Theophany. I tend to look at it more as an angel, but I am still studying the matter. But just as a prophet would begin to speak as God's Voice, so did angels.

The promise God makes with Hagar sounds very much like the promise He gave to Abram. This baby in the womb will go from one to an innumerable multitude.

Genesis 16:11 "And the angel of the LORD said unto her, Behold, thou art with child, and shalt bear a son, and shalt call his name Ishmael; because the LORD hath heard thy affliction."

God here tells Hagar the sex of the child. A son is going to be born. Notice as well that she is with child, not fetus or embryo. The unborn is often referred to as a person in Scripture. Hagar is to name the child Ishmael. With the family structure the way it was in that society, I would guess there may be an issue with Hagar doing the naming. We find both husbands and wives naming children in Scripture, but this situation was unique in that Hagar was still a servant while a wife in the family. But with angelic visitations, and visitations by God Himself being rather plentiful in the life of Abram, it is probable that Abram would believe Hagar's tale of the angel and act according to the angel's direction. And Hagar's change of demeanor would certainly lend credence to the fact that she had seen an angel.

Ishmael means God will hear, and is the name of six different people in Scripture. Now what was Hagar's affliction mentioned here? Being taken from Egypt, and possibly away from family? Being in the conundrum, not of her choosing, of bearing a child to the wealthy, whose long-term wife was still alive, and also her boss? The flight with absolutely nothing but the seed of a blessed man? All of these? More? Confusion? I do find it interesting that the only person with really no choice in this matter was Hagar. Sarai suggested, Abram acted, but Hagar was a powerless servant. It would have been the death penalty quite possibly, or at least severe punishment, for her to disobey.

Genesis 16:12 "And he will be a wild man; his hand will be against every man, and every man's hand against him; and he shall dwell in the presence of all his brethren."

God, as He is wont to do, begins to foretell Ishmael's future. The angel finds Hagar in the wilderness, and her seed will be wild. The play on words and situation is glaring. Ishmael will not only be wild, but he will be an antagonist to all. Hagar was against Sarai. Her seed will be against every man. In turn, every man's hand will be against him as well. Hagar was possibly without family. Ishmael will not be isolated, but he will dwell in the presence of his brethren. Hagar was fleeing, Ishmael will not flee.

Many extrapolate Ishmael's characteristics to his descendants as well. It is beyond the scope of this Commentary to explore any similarities between Ishmael and his descendants. The Arabs are in many cases the descendants of Ishmael.

Genesis 16:13 "And she called the name of the LORD that spake unto her, Thou God seest me: for she said, Have I also here looked after him that seeth me?"

Here we find it is the LORD, Jehovah, that was speaking with her. Many would say this is proof the angel was a Theophany. But it could have been Jehovah speaking through the angel as well. Jehovah is God. This is where we get the Name of God, Jehovah Roi, or El Roi.

Some would say Rohi. Thou God seest me. Ishmael means "God will hear." Hearing and seeing.

God had named her son. Now she names God after this attribute. She seems to be saying she wasn't looking for God, but God saw her. He came looking for her. This is also a hint and a shadow that we see so often that God still cares about the Gentiles, even when He was dealing with His chosen people.

Genesis 16:14 "Wherefore the well was called Beerlahairoi; behold, it is between Kadesh and Bered."

Beerlahairoi means "well of the Living God who seeth me." Fascinatingly enough, it will be Isaac who is found dwelling there in 26:62 and 25:11. The exact identification has not been definitively established, though there are a few possibilities that could fit the description. Some say Bered is 13 miles south of Beersheba, while others say the location is unknown. Bered means "hail," and another Bered is mentioned in the Ephraimite lineage in 1 Chronicles 7:20. Kedesh means "holy." It is first mentioned in 14:7, and most say it is the same as Kadesh-barnea. It is mentioned about 28 times in Scripture.

Genesis 16:15 "And Hagar bare Abram a son: and Abram called his son's name, which Hagar bare, Ishmael."

Abram probably got on board with the LORD's directive for Ishmael's name, since Hagar was to call him that, or Abram did it quite by prophecy. I would say the former is what happened, but it is not explicitly stated at this point. Again, as a matter of practice, we find both mothers and fathers naming children. And the children's names throughout much of the Old Testament period played such a role in the child's life through adulthood.

So Hagar goes back to Abram and Sarai. We are not told of how Hagar reconciled with Sarai, or of any of the details of the birth process. But the blessed, yet not promised, son was born.

Another factor we are not informed of is did Abram realize at this point that Ishmael was not the seed of promise? It had gone from Eliezer to Ishmael. Yet out of neither would Messiah come, who would be the Savior of the world.

Genesis 16:16 "And Abram was fourscore and six years old, when Hagar bare Ishmael to Abram."

Abram was 86 years old. This would have been approximately 1910 BC. This would have been about 438 years after the Flood of Noah.

Chapter 17

WHILE ALL SCRIPTURE is equally inspired and important, this Chapter stands out much like Chapter 15 as a pivotal Chapter in the Bible. The reestablishment of the Abrahamic Covenant will be shown here, and God once again has a very long discourse with Abram, soon to be Abraham.

Genesis 17:1 "And when Abram was ninety years old and nine, the LORD appeared to Abram, and said unto him, I am the Almighty God; walk before me, and be thou perfect."

An angel appeared unto Hagar, yet it is Jehovah God who appears to Abram. Almighty God is El Shaddai. Jesus is seen as the Almighty in Revelation 1:8. This is the first usage of the term in Scripture. El Shaddai, written by Michael Card and sung by Amy Grant, continues to be one of the best Christian songs of all time.

13 years elapse between the end of Chapter 16 and the beginning of Chapter 17. Ishmael would have been 13 at this time. In what form Jehovah appeared to Abram we are not sure. It was a vision in Chapter 15. In Chapter 18, He will appear as a Man with two angels with Him.

Jehovah telling Abram to walk before Him is telling. In 13:17 he was to walk through the land. Since God had called Abram out of Ur of the Chaldees some 24 years prior, Abram had spent much of the time walking. A stranger in a strange land. Yet one he was covenantally promised to possess. And the call to be perfect was certainly a high calling indeed. One is reminded of 2 Corinthians 6:14-7:1 and 2 Corinthians 13 in this regard. How could Abram be perfect? It seems as if God was calling Abram to a higher standard in order to seal His covenant with him.

The call to be perfect is a fascinating call. Since kind can only mate with kind (Genesis 1), and God is perfect, maybe the call to be perfect had to do with establishing a covenant out of which would come the perfect God/Man, Jesus. Perhaps two equals on a certain level had to make the covenant. Whatever the reasoning, the command to be perfect certainly stands out.

Genesis 17:2 "And I will make my covenant between me and thee, and will multiply thee exceedingly."

Verse 2 can certainly make Verse 1 sound as a dependency clause. If Abram will walk before God and be perfect, then God will make His covenant with Abram. Some, of course, would dispute this and say Verse 2 is merely a statement of fact and intent. Was the covenant conditional or unconditional? Whatever the case, God is the Initiator of the covenant. Psalm 37 is known for its conditional clauses for God's blessings. God here promises to multiply Abram exceedingly. There is still no differentiation between Ishmael and the promised seed mentioned. Notice as well it is not a covenant, but God calls it His Covenant (my covenant).

Also, it is not stated here definitively whether the increase will be solely Abram's seed, or Abram's wealth would likewise be increased. Word of Faith Preachers like Oral Roberts used Abram's wealth as a justification for wealth to be part of God's New Covenant blessings.

Genesis 17:3 "And Abram fell on his face: and God talked with him, saying,"

This Verse is often used for a justification of the Pentecostal practice of being slain in the Spirit. While this doesn't seem to be exactly congruent, being in the Presence of God certainly provokes strong reactions often in Scripture. Moses, Isaiah, and even John would evince strong emotions from being in the presence of God or angels. Elohim continues to talk with Abram.

Genesis 17:4 "As for me, behold, my covenant is with thee, and thou shalt be a father of many nations."

God emphasizes it is His covenant, and He has chosen to have this covenant with Abram. Abram is to be a father of many nations. He is the beginner of a certain group of nations. While some look at this as just the 12 Tribes of Israel, which could be referred to as Nations, Abram actually was the father of more nations than that. Ishmael would have children who in turn would become tribes and nations. Keturah would have seed from Abram after the death of Sarai, and tribes and nations would come of her. In the New Testament it seems in the expansive nature of the New Covenant that would include all people, including Gentile Nations, is also included here (Romans 4:16,17 expounds on this theme). His seed would certainly be as figuratively numerous as the sand by the sea shore and the stars of heaven. Also notice here the use of the thou shalt. When God speaks, it is done, just as in Genesis 1.

Genesis 17:5 "Neither shall thy name any more be called Abram, but thy name shall be Abraham; for a father of many nations have I made thee."

Here God changes Abram's name to Abraham. Some say in the exchanging of gifts in the covenant, that God shared an H out of His Name YHWH with Abram. Be that as it may, Abram's name meaning went from High Father, to Father of a Multitude with the expansion of his name. A fascinating study is seeing all of the people in Scripture who had their name changed by God.

Notice God made Abram a father of many nations, though he had but one 13 year old son at the time. God did not speak in the past tense, but out of His El Shaddai Almighty Nature, it was done. God can speak those things that be not as though they are. He is eternal and dwells outside of time. He observes time as a helicopter observes a parade from high above, seeing the end from the beginning.

When we enter into covenant with God, our name must be changed. This is part of the importance of Jesus' Name Baptism in our lives. As His bride, we must take His Name (see Genesis 5:2). And with that name change, we get the blessing of our Bridegroom in our lives.

Genesis 17:6 "And I will make thee exceeding fruitful, and I will make nations of thee, and kings shall come out of thee."

Abram, or now Abraham, with his face to the ground, continues to hear the voice of God. This attitude of humility may be at least part of the reason God chose him in the first place. God uses superlatives to stress the extreme blessings that are coming upon Abraham. Abraham is already fabulously blessed. But at 99 years of age, and with the natural forms of childbearing gone from both he and Sarai, God says he is just getting started. God blessing in old age and past the time of the natural is a constant refrain of Scripture. Moses and Noah come to mind. Daniel was at the end of his life being second in command in Persia and being thrown into the lion's den.

God is also looking to the future in this Verse. The language "will" means from this time forward, and "kings shall," indicates future tense. So, it is not just Ishmael who will be blessed, but the blessing of children and progeny upon Abraham is just getting started. God also begins to say that not only nations, but kings are going to come out of Abraham. Since every born again believer is a king and priest, and also the children of Abraham, we are part of that promise. The fascinating part of living beings being inside of us is really a point to ponder as well. Abraham has defeated four kings, helped five kings, had interactions with Pharaoh, now his seed will include kings, including the King of Kings and Lord of Lords.

Genesis 17:7 "And I will establish my covenant between me and thee and thy seed after thee in their generations for an everlasting covenant, to be a God unto thee, and to thy seed after thee."
God now makes it crystal clear that His covenant will extend to

Abraham's seed forever. This is an everlasting covenant. This means there will always be a natural Israel evidently, as their names, the 12 Patriarchs, are on the gates of the New Jerusalem. But it also includes the Church. So, this so-called Abrahamic Covenant is an everlasting covenant. This is why Chapter 17 is so pivotal to the remainder of Scripture. Also notice that God is going to be a God to Abraham and his seed, with all of the power and responsibilities that entails.

Genesis 17:8 "And I will give unto thee, and to thy seed after thee, the land wherein thou art a stranger, all the land of Canaan, for an everlasting possession; and I will be their God."

This now seems to be an unconditional covenant. Abraham, and all of his future seed, will get the land of Canaan in an everlasting possession. And God will be their God. Romans 11 seems to highlight this point. The great number of the Jewish people may be currently enemies of the Gospel, at least religious Jews, but they are still beloved of the Father due to the everlasting nature of this covenant. One man effected eternity. Abraham. God has not cast off his seed.

All the land of Canaan will go to Abraham, not just part. God gave the parameters earlier, from the river of Egypt to the Euphrates. It will come to pass. God has in our generation regathered Israel. This will last.

Conclusion

WE BEGAN THIS DISCUSSION in Scripture focusing on Genesis 12:16, in approximately 1921 BC. Sarai was captive in Egypt, and the fate of the world hung in the balance. We end it in the middle of God speaking at length to Abraham about the nature of His covenant with Abram. In the 92 Verses of this Commentary, we end in approximately 1897 BC. The promised seed is getting close. In these 92 Verses, we have two extended sections of God speaking with Abraham. During this discussion, the Abrahamic Covenant has been presented and confirmed. Abraham began as Abram, he has ended as Abraham. The world has been changed. Abraham has been separated from Lot. He has rescued Lot. He has defeated a Mesopotamian consortium of kings. He has met Melchizedek and given this King Priest tithes. We have been introduced to Salem, later to be called Jerusalem. We have also been introduced to Sodom and its sister cities. We need to stop here. The remainder of the Abrahamic Covenant, Abraham meeting Jehovah and the two angels, the destruction of the cities of the plain, and Abraham's life beyond seem to fit together for another volume. Better to leave this one slightly shorter than to be out of balance in the sharing of the beautiful, life-giving, Holy Scriptures. Shalom! May the grace and peace of our Lord Jesus Christ be with you!

P.S. It is rather shocking and telling that we are not yet quite to the halfway point of the Abraham narrative in Scripture, which will go on into Chapter 25, such is his importance to the Bible and life in general. The telling of his life dwarfs that of Adam and Noah and should tell us where God's interests lie.

CPSIA information can be obtained
at www.ICGtesting.com
Printed in the USA
LVHW030401270422
716686LV00002B/98